David's Mighty Men

Stories with Grandpa

This Book Belongs To:

_____

Dedicated to Liam, Caleb, & Tyler

Stories With Grandpa

Written by Josiah Fogle
Illustrated by Rozent Dumlao

Buddy's favorite weekends were the ones he got to visit his grandparents. His Grandpa always came up with the best things to do. From playing with trains and planes to making funny highlighter mustaches and more.

Most of all, Buddy loved listening to Grandpa's stories. When mom dropped Buddy off at Grandpa's house one day, she told him how Buddy had a tough night not telling the truth and fighting with his little brother. Grandpa had the perfect story to help Buddy!

"Psst, hey Buddy. It's story time!" Grandpa said to Buddy.

"Oh boy, oh boy! Grandpa, I love your stories!" Buddy replied, running to him.

"How about I tell you the story of King David's mighty men?" Grandpa asked.

"Mighty men?" questioned Buddy.

"Yes, God gave some of King David's men super strength!" Grandpa answered.

"Why did God give them super strength?" Buddy asked.

"That's a great question, Buddy! God gave them super strength because they were obeying King David. King David was following what God wanted him to do." Grandpa explained.

"God gave them super strength and the ability to do unbelievable things so that others would see how awesome God is! God gives those who follow him faithfully and with their whole hearts exactly what they need. Let me tell you about three of David's mighty men."

"One day, when David's men were fighting the bad guys, who were called the Philistines, all of David's men ran away...

All except one! His name was Eleazar. He was someone who never gave up."

 "Eleazar fought

and fought

 and fought...

until he was too tired to lift his sword! He had fought for so long that his sword became stuck to his hand from holding it so tightly. Since Eleazar had super strength, God's army won a great victory that day."

"Shamma was another one of King David's mighty men. He was special like Eleazar. When he was surrounded by the Philistines in the middle of a battlefield, he won because of God's super strength, leading King David's men to another victory."

"The third mighty man was Josheb. He fought 800 Philistines in a single battle with only a spear! He was so brave! Buddy, isn't that amazing?"

"Is God going to give me super strength so I can fight bad guys too?" Buddy wondered aloud while thinking of his favorite super hero.

"That's a great question, Buddy!" Grandpa replied with a chuckle.

"God has already given us the most special gift. It's even better than super strength! When we love and believe in Him, He gives us the Holy Spirit."

"With the Holy Spirit in your heart, you can do all of the amazing things God has planned for you. No matter what comes your way, Buddy, you can trust the Holy Spirit is with you."

"Now, you might not have a spear like Josheb, stand in the middle of the battlefield like Shamma, or have your hand stuck to your sword like Eleazar, but you do have a Helper. With Him, you can be brave!"

Buddy thought to himself for a second then asked

"Is God with me when I am afraid in a thunderstorm?"

"Yes, God is with you. He can make you super brave even in the middle of a scary storm, and He can use you to comfort others!"

"What about when it is really hard to tell the truth?" Buddy asked.

"Yes, God is with you. He gives you super courage to do the hard thing and to tell the truth."

"How is God with me when my little brother takes my toys? Can I fight him like Eleazar did?" Buddy asked, hoping Grandpa would say yes.

"No, Buddy," Grandpa chuckled. "God wants you to love your brother and to share. God will give you everything you need like super patience when you share and play with your brother."

"Thank you, Grandpa. Now I know I can be brave. Can you tell me another story?"

"Buddy, nothing gives me more joy. Maybe next time I can share the one about how to make a big difference even when you are small."

As Buddy got ready to go home he was already looking forward to the next stories with Grandpa.

Thank you for spending time with Grandpa and Buddy!

Visit www.StoriesWithGrandpa.com to download coloring pages and see additional books.

Small, But Wise

Prayer Guide For Kids

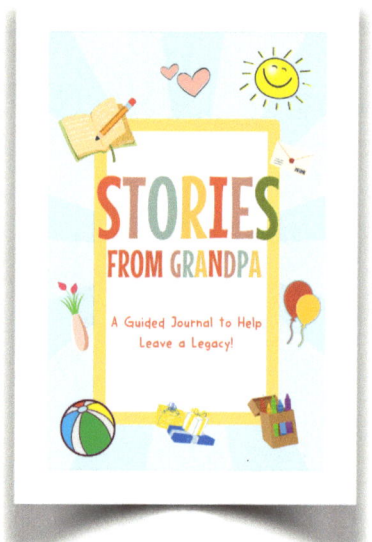

Stories From Grandpa Journal

Grandpa John

The Grandpa in this story is a testament to the life of John Fogle. Grandpa John loved Jesus and was called to be a missionary to the Philippines for many, many years. Grandpa John was an example of someone who did not grow up knowing Jesus, but came to know God through someone sharing with him. He then, like Eleazar, held firm to his sword, the Word of God, until he went home to be with Jesus in October 2016. God used him to impact thousands and thousands of people through the ministry of Word of Life Philippines. John started with no seminary degree or formal theological training. Over time he ended up becoming the Academic Dean at the Word of Life Bible Institute as well as a respected speaker and very skilled teacher of the Bible. He was someone who took the Great Commission seriously. Even when facing cancer and coming to the end of his life, he prayed desperately for opportunities to share Jesus with his doctor and nurses, one of whom has a relationship with Jesus now. For anyone who knew him, that story is not surprising; Grandpa John's love of Jesus was obvious.

Stories With Grandpa is a collection of stories designed to honor the memory of Grandpa John but more importantly point to God and give Him the Glory.

My prayer is that through reading this book you will be encouraged. If there is anything I can pray for, or if you want to know more about Jesus and what a relationship with Him is all about email me at josiahfogle@gmail.com

NOW IT'S YOUR TURN
Want to get your story PUBLISHED?

Self-Publishing School helped me, and now I want them to help you with this FREE resource to begin outlining your book!

Even if you're busy, bad at writing, or don't know where to start, you CAN write a bestseller and build your best life.

With tools and experience across a variety of niches and professions, Self-Publishing School is the only resource you need to take your book to the finish line!

DON'T WAIT

Say "YES" to telling your story!
https://self-publishingschool.com/friend/

Follow the steps on the page to get a FREE resource to get started on your book and unlock a discount to get started with Self-Publishing School.

Fogleworks© Copyright 2021 Josiah Fogle
Illustrations by Rozent Dumlao
ISBN-13: 978-1-7379064-0-7

Copyright notice: All rights reserved. No part of this book may be reproduced or transmitted in any form or by any means, electronic or mechanical, including photocopying and recording, or by any information storage and retrieval system, without permission in writing from the author.

For more information, email josiahfogle@gmail.com

www.ingramcontent.com/pod-product-compliance
Lightning Source LLC
Chambersburg PA
CBHW061400090426
42743CB00002B/93